W9-CSR-505

C L A S S I C S

Great American

Short Stories I

❦

Washington
IRVING

Stories retold by Joanne Suter
Illustrated by Tracy Hall

LAKE EDUCATION
Belmont, California

LAKE CLASSICS

Great American Short Stories I

Washington Irving, Nathaniel Hawthorne, Mark Twain, Bret
Harte, Edgar Allan Poe, Kate Chopin, Willa Cather, Sarah
Orne Jewett, Sherwood Anderson, Charles W. Chesnutt

Great American Short Stories II

Herman Melville, Stephen Crane, Ambrose Bierce, Jack
London, Edith Wharton, Charlotte Perkins Gilman, Frank R.
Stockton, Hamlin Garland, O. Henry, Richard Harding Davis

Great British and Irish Short Stories

Arthur Conan Doyle, Saki (H. H. Munro), Rudyard Kipling,
Katherine Mansfield, Thomas Hardy, E. M. Forster, Robert
Louis Stevenson, H. G. Wells, John Galsworthy, James Joyce

Great Short Stories from Around the World

Guy de Maupassant, Anton Chekhov, Leo Tolstoy, Selma
Lagerlöf, Alphonse Daudet, Mori Ogwai, Leopoldo Alas,
Rabindranath Tagore, Fyodor Dostoevsky, Honoré de Balzac

Cover and Text Designer: Diann Abbott

Library of Congress Catalog Number: 94-075012
ISBN 1-56103-002-3
Printed in the United States of America
1 9 8 7 6 5 4 3 2 1

CONTENTS

❧ Lake Classic Short Stories ❧

"The universe is made of stories, not atoms."
—Muriel Rukeyser

"The story's about you."
—Horace

Everyone loves a good story. It is hard to think of a friendlier introduction to classic literature. For one thing, short stories are *short*—quick to get into and easy to finish. Of all the literary forms, the short story is the least intimidating and the most approachable.

Great literature is an important part of our human heritage. In the belief that this heritage belongs to everyone, *Lake Classic Short Stories* are adapted for today's readers. Lengthy sentences and paragraphs are shortened. Archaic words are replaced. Modern punctuation and spellings are used. Many of the longer stories are abridged. In all the stories, painstaking care has been taken to preserve the author's unique voice.

Lake Classic Short Stories have something for everyone. The hundreds of stories in the collection cover a broad terrain of themes, story types, and styles. Literary merit was a deciding factor in story selection. But no story was included unless it was as enjoyable as it was instructive. And special priority was given to stories that shine light on the human condition.

Each book in the *Lake Classic Short Stories* is devoted to the work of a single author. Little-known stories of merit are included with famous old favorites. Taken as a whole, the collected authors and stories make up a rich and diverse sampler of the story-teller's art.

Lake Classic Short Stories guarantee a great reading experience. Readers who look for common interests, concerns, and experiences are sure to find them. Readers who bring their own gifts of perception and appreciation to the stories will be doubly rewarded.

❧ Washington Irving ❧
(1783–1859)

About the Author

Washington Irving was the youngest and most gifted child in a large, well-to-do family. He lived during the years between the Revolutionary War and the Civil War.

As a youth, Irving read a great deal and wrote poems, plays, and essays for children. He studied law and was admitted to the bar, but he never practiced as a lawyer.

By the time he was 19, Irving was writing sketches under the name "Jonathan Oldstyle." These sketches were about society and the theater of New York City. They were published in a New York newspaper edited by his brother Peter.

Irving was a man of medium height with chestnut hair and blue eyes. He was said to have a pleasant, husky voice. Charles Dickens, the great English novelist, once described Irving's laugh. He called it "that captivating laugh of his, which was the brightest and best I have ever heard."

Irving's *History of New York by Diedrich Knickerbocker* was America's first remarkable piece of comic literature. It was said that "old New York shook with a roar of laughter" after it was published in 1809. This book marked the beginning of the "Knickerbocker School" of New York writers. These writers took their name and humorous tone from Irving.

In 1820, Irving published *The Sketch Book of Geoffrey Crayon, Gent*. In this book were the two stories for which he is best remembered: "Rip Van Winkle" and "The Legend of Sleepy Hollow." Irving was the first real comedian in American literature. Even today's readers find it hard not to laugh at Ichabod Crane and some of the other funny characters he created.

Rip Van Winkle

How could a man's beard grow so long in just one night? How did his gun get so rusty? Meet Rip Van Winkle—one of the most famous characters in American literature.

EVEN IN THIS FAVORITE PLACE, THE UNLUCKY RIP WAS
HUNTED DOWN BY HIS WIFE.

Rip Van Winkle

Whoever has sailed up the Hudson River must remember the Catskill Mountains. They are a part of the great Appalachian range. They rise up west of the river and tower over the countryside. Every change of season, every change of weather—indeed, every hour of the day—changes the color and shape of these mountains.

It is almost like magic. When the weather is fair and the sky settled, the mountains are clothed in blue and purple. Yet sometimes, when the rest of the sky is clear, the mountaintops wear a gray hood of fog. In the last rays of the setting sun, this fog lights up like a crown of glory.

At the foot of these fairy mountains, smoke curls up from a village. Pointed roofs gleam among the trees. The little village is very old. It was founded long ago by Dutch colonists. A few of the first settlers' houses still stand. They are built of small yellow bricks brought over from Holland.

Long ago, in one of these very houses, lived a simple, good-natured fellow by the name of Rip Van Winkle. Even then, his house was sadly time-worn and weather-beaten. Rip was a kind neighbor and a gentle, henpecked husband. Indeed, the kindness of nature made him very popular in the village.

It is certain that he was a great favorite among all the good wives of the village. They always took his side in family quarrels and never failed to lay the blame on Dame Van Winkle. The children of the village, too, would shout with joy when he came around. He made them toys, taught them to fly kites, and told them ghost stories. Wherever he went about the village, he was circled by a group of children. They hung on his clothing and climbed on his back. Not even a dog would bark at him in all the neighborhood.

Rip had one big fault. He stayed away from any kind of paying work. It was not because he could not put his mind to things. He could sit on a rock and fish all day—even though he might not get a single bite. He could carry his gun on his shoulder for hours, marching through woods and swamps. But he only did this if he wanted to shoot a few squirrels.

Rip only worked when he wanted to. He would never refuse to help a neighbor—even with the hardest work. Often the women of the village asked him to do little jobs their own husbands would not do. In a word, Rip was ready to take care of anybody's business but his own. As to keeping his own farm in order—he found it impossible.

In fact, he often said that it was no use at all to work on his farm. It was the worst piece of ground in the whole country, he said. Everything about it went wrong—and *would* go wrong in spite of him. His fences were falling to pieces. His cow often ran away. Rain always started to fall just as he began some outside work. So his farm had fallen apart, bit by bit. Finally, there was little left but a patch of corn and potatoes. It was the most run-down place in the neighborhood.

His children, too, were ragged and wild. They looked like they belonged to nobody. His son Rip looked just like him. And it appeared likely that young Rip would grow up with the same habits. The boy was often seen playing at his mother's heels. Often he wore an old pair of his father's pants which he held up with one hand.

Rip Van Winkle, however, was a happy man. He took the world easy, eating white bread or brown, whichever could be got with the least thought or trouble.

If left to himself, he would have cheerfully whistled his life away. But his wife kept nagging about his laziness and his carelessness. She said he was bringing ruin on his family.

Morning, noon, and night her mouth was going. Rip had just one way of answering her scoldings. He shook his head and looked up at the sky—but said nothing. This usually brought on more angry words from his wife. Then Rip would go outside of the house. Outside is the only side that truly belongs to a henpecked husband.

Rip had a dog named Wolf. Poor Wolf was as henpecked as his master. Dame Van Winkle saw the man and his dog as friends in laziness. The moment Wolf entered the house, his tail dropped to the ground or curled beneath his legs.

As their years of marriage rolled on, things grew worse and worse for Rip Van Winkle. A bad temper never gets better with age. A sharp tongue is the only tool that grows sharper with use. For a long while he would escape from his home to the bench at the village inn. There he would join a few other idle fellows of the village. Hour after hour they would sit in the shade on a long, lazy summer's day. Near the front door of the inn was a picture of His Majesty, King George the Third. Just underneath that picture, they would talk over village news or tell endless, sleepy stories about nothing.

But even in this favorite place, the unlucky Rip was hunted down by his wife. She would suddenly break in upon the peaceful gathering. Then she would scold *all* the members of the group for their lazy habits.

Poor Rip's only real escape from the scoldings was to take gun in hand and go away into the woods. There he would sometimes seat himself at the foot of a tree and talk with Wolf.

"Poor Wolf," he would say, "thy mistress makes it a dog's life, for sure. But never mind! While I live, thou shalt never want a friend to stand by thee!" Wolf would wag his tail and look hopefully at his master's face.

Rip took one of these walks on a fine fall day. Before he knew it, he had climbed to one of the highest parts of the Catskill Mountains. He was after his favorite sport—squirrel-shooting. For a long while, the silent, lonely woods had echoed with his gunshots. But by late afternoon, he was panting and tired. He threw himself down on the top of a green hill. From an opening between the trees, he could look over the rich woodland in the valley. At a distance he could see the mighty Hudson River far, far below him.

On the other side, he looked down into a deep mountain glen. It was wild, lonely, and barely lit by the rays of the setting sun. Evening was coming. The tall mountains began to throw their long, blue shadows over the valleys. Rip saw that it would be dark long before he could reach the village. He sighed when he thought of returning home to the angry Dame Van Winkle.

As he was about to start down the hill, he heard a voice. It was calling from the distance, "Rip Van Winkle! Rip Van

Winkle!" He looked around. He saw
nothing but a crow winging its way
across the mountain. Thinking he must
have imagined the voice, he turned again
to go down. But then he heard the same
cry ringing through the still evening air.
"Rip Van Winkle! Rip Van Winkle!" the
voice called out. At the same time the
hair stood up on Wolf's back.

Rip began to feel just a bit frightened.
He looked down into the glen. There he
saw a figure slowly climbing up the
rocks. The man seemed to be bending
under the weight of something he carried
on his back. Rip was surprised to see any
human being in this lonely place. He
supposed it was some neighbor, so he
hurried down to help him.

Coming closer, Rip was still more
surprised at the way the stranger looked.
He was a short, square-built old fellow.
He had thick bushy hair and a beard. The
stranger's clothing seemed to come from
the days of old. He wore several pairs of
pants. The outer pair was very large.

The strange little man carried a round keg on his shoulder. He made signs for Rip to come closer—as if he needed help with the load. Though rather shy, Rip went to lend a hand. Taking turns carrying the heavy keg, they made their way across the dry bed of a mountain stream.

As they walked, Rip began to hear long rolling sounds, like far-off thunder. The noise seemed to come from a deep pass between some high rocks. He stopped to listen for a moment. But then he decided that it was a distant mountain storm, so he went on. At last they came to a hollow circled by trees. The place was like a small, outdoor theater. The thick tree branches almost shut out the sky and the bright evening clouds. During this whole time Rip and the stranger had not said a word to each other.

New wonders presented themselves as they entered the hollow. On a flat spot in the middle, a group of strange-looking fellows were bowling. They were dressed in very odd, old-fashioned clothing. Some wore short jackets and others wore vests, with long knives in their belts. Most of the men wore huge pants.

Their faces, too, were quite odd. One had a large beard, a wide face, and small pig-like eyes. The face of another seemed to be all one big nose. This giant nose peeked out from under a tall, white hat that was topped with a little red feather. All the little men had beards of different shapes and colors.

One man seemed to be the leader. He was a stout old gentleman with a lined face. He wore a laced jacket, a wide belt, and a high hat with a feather. He also wore red stockings, and high-heeled shoes with roses on them.

The whole group made Rip think of an old painting he had seen. These men looked like the figures in that picture that had been brought from Holland.

Rip noticed how serious these people looked—even though they seemed to be at play. They were completely silent. Nothing broke the quiet but the noise of the rolling balls. Whenever the balls were rolled, the sound echoed along the mountains like claps of thunder.

Rip and the man with the keg made their way up to the group. Suddenly, the bowlers stopped their play and stared at him. They watched Rip without moving, and their faces showed no feeling. Rip's heart pounded and his knees began to knock together. The short man now emptied his keg into some large bottles. He made signs for Rip to wait. Rip obeyed, shaking with fear. The fellows drank from the bottles in silence. Then they returned to their game.

Little by little, Rip's fears disappeared. When no one was looking, he even tasted the drink. He found it quite good. Rip was always a thirsty fellow, so he soon took another drink. One taste led to another. He made many visits to the bottle. In time, his eyes swam in his head, his head dropped to his chest, and he fell into a deep sleep.

On waking, Rip found himself on the green hill where he had first seen the old man with the keg. He rubbed his eyes. It was a bright, sunny morning. The birds were singing.

"Surely," thought Rip, "I have not slept here all night." He remembered what had happened before he fell asleep. He thought of the strange man with the keg, the mountain pass, and the silent bowling party. Then he remembered the bottle. "Oh! That bottle! That wicked bottle!" thought Rip. "What shall I say to Dame Van Winkle?"

He looked around for his gun. But in place of his clean, well-oiled gun, he found an old one lying beside him. The barrel was covered with rust. The lock was falling off. The handle was worm-eaten. He now suspected that the bowlers of the mountain had tricked him and robbed him of his gun. Wolf, too, had disappeared. He whistled for the dog and shouted his name. But Wolf was nowhere to be seen.

Rip decided to go back to the spot of last night's party. If he met any of the group, he would ask for his gun and his dog. But when he got to his feet, he found himself very stiff and sore. He did not have his usual energy.

"These mountain beds do not agree with me," thought Rip. With some work, he got down into the pass. He found the path that he and the little man had taken the evening before. But, to his surprise, a mountain stream now ran down the path. Slowly, Rip worked his way through bushes and weeds. From time to time he tripped on the wild vines that hung from tree to tree.

At last he reached the place where the path had opened to the hollow. But no trace of that hollow was there now! At the place it should have been, a waterfall came tumbling over a high wall of rocks. Poor Rip just stood there. Again he called and whistled for his dog. But the only answer he got was the calling of crows.

What was to be done? The morning was passing away. Rip was hungry for his breakfast. He hated to leave the mountain without his dog and gun. And he surely did not look forward to meeting his wife. But it would not do to starve. He shook his head and shouldered the rusty gun. With a heart full of worry, he turned his steps toward home.

As he neared the village, he passed a number of people. Not one of them did he know. This surprised him—for he thought he knew everyone in that part of the country. Their clothing, too, was different from what he was used to. They all looked at him with just as much surprise. Whenever they turned their eyes upon him, they rubbed their chins. After a bit, Rip reached up and rubbed his own. He found his beard had grown a foot long!

Now he entered the edge of the village. A parade of strange children ran at his heels. They called after him and pointed at his gray beard. The dogs, too, barked at him as he passed. Not one of them did he know as an old friend!

The very village was changed. It was larger now, and many more people seemed to live there. There were rows of houses that he had never seen before.

Strange names were over the doors, strange faces at the windows. Everything was strange.

Rip began to wonder if some magic was at work. Surely this was his own village, which he had left only the day before. He rubbed his eyes and looked around. There stood the Catskill Mountains. There ran the silver Hudson. There was every hill, just where it had always been. Rip did not understand. "That bottle last night," he thought, "has surely confused me!"

It was with some trouble that he found the way to his own house. He went toward it silently, waiting to hear the high voice of Dame Van Winkle. As he came nearer, he saw that the house was in sad shape. The roof had fallen in. The windows were all broken. A thin, unhappy dog that looked like Wolf was creeping about it. Rip called him by name, but the dog growled, showed his teeth, and passed on. This was a blow indeed. "My own dog," cried poor Rip, "has forgotten me!"

He went into the house, which Dame
Van Winkle had always kept in good
order. But it was empty—as if no one
lived there. Rip felt very much alone. He
called loudly to his wife and children.
For a moment the empty room rang with
his voice. Then all was silent.

Now Rip hurried to the village inn. It
was not there, either. A large wooden
building stood in its place. Over its door
was painted "The Union Hotel." The
picture of King George was gone. Instead
there was a picture of a man in a blue
coat. Underneath, the name "George
Washington" was painted in large letters.

The great tree that once shaded the
quiet village inn was gone, too. Now in
its place there stood a tall pole. Something that looked like a nightcap was
flying from the top. The cloth was covered
with stars and stripes. All of this was
strange and impossible to understand.

There was, as usual, a crowd of folk
about the door. But Rip remembered not
one of them. The people seemed different.

There was a busy, hurried tone about them instead of the usual sleepy quiet. A thin, tall fellow was handing out papers to everyone. He was shouting loudly about the rights of citizens, liberty, Bunker Hill, and the heroes of '76. All of these words were nonsense to the confused Van Winkle.

Rip's long beard, rusty gun, and strange dress began to draw attention. One old gentleman in a high hat made his way through the crowd. He planted himself before Rip and shouted at him. "Why did you come to the election with a gun on your shoulder? Do you mean to start trouble in the village?"

"Alas! Gentlemen," cried Rip, "I am a poor, quiet man—born in this place—and a loyal subject of the king!"

Here a great shout came from the crowd. "A Tory! A Tory! A spy! Away with him!"

The gentleman in the high hat called for order. Again he asked Rip where he came from and what he wanted. Poor Rip said that he meant no harm, but was only looking for some of his neighbors.

"Well—who are they? Name them," the gentleman said.

Rip thought a moment. Then he asked, "Where is Nicholas Vedder?"

There was a silence for a little while. Then an old man answered, "Nicholas Vedder? Why, he is dead and gone these 18 years! There was once a wood marker in the churchyard that told all about him. But that is gone now, too."

"Where is Brom Dutcher?" asked Rip.

"Oh, he went off to the army at the beginning of the war. Some say he was killed. I don't know. He never came back."

"Where's Van Bummel, the school teacher?"

"He went off to the war, too. Now he is in Congress."

Rip's heart sank. Hearing of these sad changes in his village made him very unhappy. He missed his home and his friends. Just one night away—and now he was alone in the world. Every answer puzzled him. How had so much time gone by? What was all this talk of war and Congress? He was afraid to ask about any more friends. He cried out, "Does nobody here know Rip Van Winkle?"

"Oh, Rip Van Winkle!" cried two or three of the people. "Oh, to be sure! That's Rip Van Winkle over there, leaning against the tree."

Rip looked. He saw an exact copy of himself as he was when he went up the mountain. The young fellow seemed just as lazy and certainly as ragged. Poor Rip was more confused than ever. He was no longer sure if he was himself or if he was another man. Then suddenly the man in the tall hat demanded to know his name.

"God knows!" Rip cried. "I am not myself. I'm somebody else. That's me over there. No, that's somebody else standing in my shoes. I was myself last night—but I fell asleep on the mountain. They have changed my gun, and now *everything* has changed. *I'm* changed, and I can't tell who I am!"

Now the people of the village began to look at each other. They nodded and winked and tapped their fingers against their heads. They started to whisper about getting the gun before the old fellow could do any harm.

Just then a fresh, pretty woman pressed through the crowd. She peeked at the gray-bearded man around the baby she carried in her arms. Frightened by his looks, the child began to cry. "Hush, Rip," she whispered. "The old man won't hurt you." The name of the child, the face of the mother, the sound of her voice, all caught Rip Van Winkle's notice.

"What is your name, my good woman?" asked he.

"Judith Gardenier."

"And your father's name?"

"Ah, poor man, Rip Van Winkle was his name. But it's 20 years since he went away from home. He went off with his gun and has never been heard of since. His dog came home without him. But whether he shot himself or was carried away by wild animals—nobody can tell. I was then but a little girl."

Rip had just one more question to ask. "Where is your mother?"

"Oh, she too died but a short time ago. She broke a blood vessel in an angry fit at a New England peddler," the young woman answered.

Rip found a drop of comfort, at least, in this news. The honest man could hold back no longer. He caught his daughter and her child in his arms. "I am your father!" cried he. "Young Rip Van Winkle once—old Rip Van Winkle now! Does nobody know poor Rip Van Winkle?"

All stood staring, until an old woman came out from among the crowd. She shaded her eyes with her hand and looked closely at his face for a moment. Then she cried, "Sure enough! It *is* Rip Van Winkle! It is himself! Welcome home again, old neighbor. Why, where have you been these 20 long years?"

Rip's story was soon told. The whole 20 years had seemed to him as just one night. The neighbors' eyes opened wide when they heard his tale. Many shook their heads and frowned.

It was decided to take up the matter with old Peter Vanderdonk, the oldest person in the village. He remembered Rip at once. He told everyone that the Catskill Mountains had always been haunted by strange beings. It was a fact, he said, handed down over the years.

Indeed, the ghost of Hendrick Hudson, the man who discovered the river, came back there every 20 years. He and his crew kept an eye upon the river, the old man explained. Peter's father had even seen them once. They were wearing old Dutch clothing and were bowling in a hollow of the mountain. Why, he himself had heard them, one summer afternoon. The sound of their bowling balls, like far-off claps of thunder, had been just as clear as a bell.

To make a long story short, the crowd broke up. They returned to their election. Rip's daughter took him home to live with her. She had a comfortable house and a strong, cheerful farmer for a husband. Rip remembered the farmer as one of the boys who used to follow him through the village. Rip's son, who was the copy of himself he saw in the village, was hired to work on the farm. But, to no one's surprise, young Rip kept busy with anything but his work.

Slowly Rip went back to his old walks and his old ways. Soon he found a few of his old neighbors, though they were a little the worse for the wear and tear of time. And Rip soon made friends among the younger people of the town. With them he quickly became a favorite.

Rip had nothing to do at home. He had arrived at that happy age where a man can do something or nothing—just as he pleases. So he took his place once more on the bench at the inn door. There he told stories of the old times, "before the war."

It was some time before he could understand all the strange things that had happened during his sleep. There had been a Revolutionary War and the country had freed itself from the rule of old England. Instead of being a subject of King George the Third, he was now a free citizen of the United States.

But Rip, in fact, was not interested in politics. The changes of states mattered little to him. There was just one freedom that he was happy to find. He was no longer under the hand of Dame Van Winkle. Now, he could go in and out and back and forth whenever he pleased. Any time her name was mentioned, he shook his head and looked up at the sky.

Rip used to tell his story to every stranger who came to the Union Hotel. There was not a man, woman, or child in the neighborhood who didn't know it by heart. Some pretended to doubt that the story was true. They said that Rip had been out of his head.

The old Dutch of the village, however, stood by Rip's story. Even to this day, they always say the same thing when they hear a thunder storm on a summer afternoon. They say that Hendrick Hudson and his crew are bowling.

And there is still a common wish among all henpecked husbands. When life hangs heavy on their hands, they wish that they might have a quieting drink out of Rip Van Winkle's bottle.

The Devil and Tom Walker

Why would anyone make a deal with the devil? In this story a man's greed leads him into a bad bargain. What happens when his debt comes due?

"THIS WOODLAND BELONGED TO ME LONG BEFORE ANY
OF YOU PUT FOOT UPON THE SOIL!"

The Devil and Tom Walker

A few miles away from Boston in Massachusetts, there is a deep finger of water. It runs out of Charles Bay and winds several miles into the country. It ends at last in a thickly wooded swamp. On one side of the water is a beautiful dark stand of trees. On the other side, the land rises quickly from the water's edge into a high ridge. A few scattered oaks of great age and giant size grow there.

Under one of these huge trees—as the old stories go—a great treasure was buried by Kidd the pirate. The waterway made it easy to bring the money there in a boat—secretly at night. The rise of land served as a fine lookout. And the big trees were good landmarks to help the pirates easily find the place again.

The old stories also say that the devil was present at the hiding of the money. In fact, he became its special guard. But it is well known that the devil always stays close to buried treasure—especially when it has been gotten by wicked means. Be that as it may, the pirate Kidd was arrested in Boston shortly after the treasure was buried. He was sent to England and hanged there as a thieving pirate. He never returned to dig up his treasure.

About the year 1727, earthquakes shook the land around New England. Those who had done wrong trembled with fear and fell to their knees. One man who lived there was a tight, penny-

pinching fellow by the name of Tom
Walker. There were very few good points
about Tom Walker at all. And he had a
wife as cheap with money as he was
himself. They were so stingy that they
even tried to cheat each other.

Whatever the woman could lay hands
on, she hid away. A hen could not cackle
before she was there to get the newly laid
egg for herself. Her husband was always
looking about for the secret spots where
she hid her money.

Loud and many were the fights in that
house. It was a sad-looking cottage that
stood all alone. Only a few thin trees
grew nearby. No smoke curled from its
chimney. No traveler ever stopped at its
door for a bit of rest. An unhappy horse,
whose ribs stuck out like iron bars,
limped about the field there. He was
always trying to find something to eat.
Sometimes he would lean his head over
the fence and look sadly at the people
passing by. He seemed to beg to be saved
from this land of hunger.

The house and the people who lived there had a bad name. Tom's wife was a tall, nagging woman. She had a quick temper, a loud mouth, and a strong arm. Her voice was often heard in a battle of words with her husband. And Tom's face sometimes showed signs that their fights became more than words. No one bothered them. The lonely traveler stayed away from the noise. He hurried on his way—happy, if he was not married, that he lived alone.

One day Tom Walker had been off to a distant part of the countryside. He took what he thought was a short cut home. The way led him through the swamp. Like most short cuts, it was a poorly chosen path. The swamp was thickly grown with gloomy trees, some of them as much as 90 feet high. Although it was only noon, the light in the swamp was very dim.

In the swamp, pits and quicksand were partly covered with green weeds and mosses. This often tricked travelers into stepping into the smothering black mud.

There were dark, silent pools there, too. These were home to the bull-frog and the water-snake. Trunks of trees lay half-drowned and half-rotting. They looked like alligators sleeping in the mud.

Tom picked his way carefully through this tricky land. He stepped slowly. Now and then he was startled by the sudden screaming of an owl or the quacking of a wild duck. At length he arrived at a firm piece of ground. This strip of land ran out like an arm into the deep heart of the swamp. Long ago Indians had lived in this area. During their wars with the first colonists, they had thought of the place as impossible to attack. So they had built a fort there to keep their women and children safe. Now nothing was left of the old Indian fort but a few walls. And these walls were slowly sinking into the ground.

Darkness was already falling when Tom Walker reached the old fort. He stopped there a while to rest himself. Anyone but he would have passed by that lonely, sad place. From stories handed down from the time of the wars, it was thought to be haunted.

Tom Walker, however, was not a man to be troubled with fears of any kind. He rested for some time on the trunk of a fallen tree. For a few minutes, he listened to the cry of a tree-toad and poked his walking stick into the black mud. Then suddenly his stick struck against something hard. He bent down and dug at the ground. And lo! A human skull lay before him. Most likely it was all that was left of a sad struggle between the Indian warriors and their enemies.

"Humph!" said Tom Walker. He gave the skull a kick to shake the dirt from it.

"Leave that skull alone!" said a deep voice. Tom lifted his eyes. A big man in a dark cloak was seated directly across from him on the stump of a tree. Tom Walker was quite surprised. He had not heard anyone arrive.

Now Tom saw that the figure had a red belt tied round his body. He also noticed that the stranger's face looked dirty—as if darkened with ashes. It seemed, perhaps, that the man had been working among fires. Thick black hair stood out from his head in all directions. He carried an ax on his shoulder.

The big man frowned at Tom and stared at him with a pair of great red eyes.

"What are you doing on my grounds?" said the man, in a heavy, growling voice.

"*Your* grounds!" said Tom. "These are no more your grounds than mine. They belong to Deacon Peabody."

"Deacon Peabody!" snarled the big stranger. "Deacon Peabody better look more to his own sins and less to those of his neighbors. Look yonder and see how Deacon Peabody is doing."

Tom looked in the direction that the stranger pointed. He saw one of the great tall trees—strong and healthy on the outside, but rotten at the heart. It had been cut nearly through, so that the first high wind was likely to blow it down.

The name of Deacon Peabody was carved on the bark of the tree. How strange! Deacon Peabody held a high place among his neighbors. But he had made his riches by driving dishonest bargains with the Indians.

Now Tom looked around quickly. He saw that most of the tall trees wore the name of some great man of the colony. All had been partly cut by the ax. The stump on which he sat was just next to a fallen tree. That tree bore the name of Crowninshield. Tom remembered a rich man of that name. It was whispered of Crowninshield that he had gotten his money by stealing.

"He's just ready for burning!" growled the cloaked man with a smile. "You see that I am quite likely to have plenty of firewood for winter."

"But what right have you," said Tom, "to cut down Deacon Peabody's trees?"

"I was here first," said the other. "This woodland belonged to me long before any of you put foot upon the soil!"

"And pray, who are you, if I may be so bold?" asked Tom.

"Oh, I go by many names," the dark stranger said. "I am called 'the wild huntsman' in some countries and 'the great miner' in several others. In this neighborhood I am known as 'the dark woodsman.' I am the friend of slave-dealers and the grand-master of the Salem witches."

"If I am not mistaken," said Tom, calmly, "this means that you are the one most often called 'Old Scratch.'"

"The same—and at your service!" replied the man, with a nod.

Such was the beginning of the meeting, as the old story goes. It all seems, however, a little too friendly to believe. Surely, to meet with such a strange person in this wild place would have shaken any man. But Tom was a hard-minded fellow. He was not easily frightened. Indeed, he had lived so long with a nagging wife that he did not even fear the devil.

It is said that the two of them went on to have a long, serious talk. They walked together as Tom returned home. The cloaked man told him of the fortune buried on the ridge by Kidd the pirate.

He said that all of this buried treasure was under his rule and protected by his power.

The stranger offered to place all of these treasures within Tom Walker's reach—because he had taken a special liking to him. But the money was to be had only on certain terms. Just what these terms were may be easily guessed, though Tom never told them out loud. But they must have been very hard, for he needed time to think them over. And Tom Walker was not a man to move slowly when money was in sight. When they reached the edge of the swamp, the stranger stopped.

"What proof have I that what you have been telling me is true?" asked Tom.

The man pressed his finger on Tom's forehead. "There! I have signed my name!" said the cloaked man. So saying, he turned away and walked into the thickest part of the swamp. As Tom said later, he seemed to go down, down, down into the earth. Soon nothing but his head and shoulders could be seen.

Then the man in the dark cloak totally disappeared.

Finally Tom reached home. Looking into a mirror, he found the black print of a finger burned into his forehead. Nothing could wash it away.

The first news his wife had to tell him was of the sudden death of Absalom Crowninshield.

Tom remembered the tree with Crowninshield's name on it. His strange friend had just cut it down. He had said it was ready for burning. "Let the thief roast," said Tom. "Who cares!" But now he felt sure that all he had heard and seen was true.

Tom did not usually tell his wife any of his secrets. But this was such an uneasy secret that he shared it with her. All of her greed was awakened at the mention of hidden gold. She ordered her husband to agree to the terms and make them both rich.

Now, Tom might have been willing to sell himself to the devil for his own reasons. But he was surely not going to do it to please his wife. So he flatly refused. Many and ugly were the fights they had over the matter. The more she talked, the more stubborn Tom became. Nothing could make him sell his soul to please her.

At last Tom's wife decided to drive the bargain alone. If the devil would agree, she would keep all the treasure for herself. Being as mean as her husband, she had as little fear as he did. So she set off alone for the old Indian fort toward the end of a summer's day. She was gone many hours.

When she came back she was quiet and angry. She told Tom about a cloaked man whom she had met about twilight. When she saw him, he was cutting at the root of a tall tree. The man was unfriendly, however. He would not make a bargain. She said she was planning to go there again, taking something to offer him this time. Just what she would take, she would not say.

The next evening Tom's wife again set off for the swamp. Her apron was full

with something heavy. Tom waited and
waited for her to come back. Midnight
came, but she did not return. Morning
passed, then noon. When night returned,
she still had not come home. Now Tom
grew uneasy. He was especially nervous
when he found she had carried off the
silver teapot and spoons, as well as
everything else of any worth.

Another night had passed. Another
morning came. No wife appeared. In a
word, she was never heard of again.

What really happened to her, nobody
knows. Many pretend to know, however. It is one of those stories that has
many endings.

Some say that she lost her way in the
swamp and sank into a deep pit. Others
whisper that she ran off with another
fellow, taking all of Tom's household
goods. Still others believe that the
stranger tricked her into some quicksand. They say her hat was found lying
on top of just such a pit.

To back this story, they say that they
saw a great, cloaked man with an ax on

his shoulder. It was late when they saw him coming out of the swamp. He carried a bundle tied in a checkered apron, they say. And he wore a big smile on his face.

The most likely story, however, says that Tom Walker grew very worried about his property. So worried, in fact, that he set out for the Indian fort. For a long afternoon he searched about the gloomy place. But his wife was nowhere to be seen. He called her name again and again. But no one answered. The only sound was a bullfrog croaking sadly from a mossy pool.

Just at the brown hour of twilight, the story goes, the owls began to hoot and the bats began to fly about. It was then that Tom heard some noise. He saw a crowd of crows circling above a tree. Caught in the branches of the tree was a bundle tied in a checkered apron. A great vulture sat beside the bundle, as if keeping watch over it. Tom leaped with joy. He knew his wife's apron, and he was sure it held his goods.

"Just let me get back my property," he said to himself, "and I will try to do without the woman."

He climbed up the tree. The vulture spread its wide wings. It sailed off screaming into the deep shadows of the forest. Tom took hold of the checkered apron. But, alas! He found nothing in it but a human heart and a liver!

As this old story goes, nothing more was ever found of Tom's wife. She had probably tried to deal with the stranger as she had been used to dealing with her husband. A nagging woman is often said to be a match for the devil. But in this case, she appears to have gotten the worst of it.

Tom told himself that he could do without his property—and certainly without his wife. He even felt a bit like thanking the dark woodsman. In the long run the man had done him a kindness. Tom went on looking for the dark stranger, but he did not find him for some time.

Whatever people may think, the devil is not always to be had for calling. He knows how to play a game or two.

After a time, it is said, Tom had grown more eager. Rather than give up the promised treasure, he was prepared to agree to anything. He met the stranger again one evening. The man wore his usual black cloak. His woodsman's ax was on his shoulder. When Tom saw him, he was walking along the swamp, humming a song. He pretended to care little about Tom. He made short answers whenever Tom questioned him, and went on humming his song.

After a bit, however, Tom brought him to business. They began to talk about the terms on which Tom was to have the pirate's treasure.

There was one condition that need not be mentioned. That condition is understood in all cases where the devil grants favors.

But there were other terms about which the woodsman was firm. He said that the money must be used in his service. Perhaps Tom could use it, he said, to send out a slave-ship. This, however, Tom refused. He knew that he was bad enough in most ways—but the devil himself could not get him to become a slave-trader.

The woodsman did not insist. Instead, he suggested that Tom should become a money-lender. The dark woodsman was always happy to see more money-lenders.

To this, Tom did not say no. In fact, that work seemed just to his taste.

"You shall open a shop in Boston next month," said the cloaked man.

"I'll do it tomorrow, if you wish," said Tom Walker.

"You shall see that people lose all their money. You must take their homes if they cannot pay their mortgages. And you must use force to collect fees."

"I'll drive them to the devil!" cried Tom Walker.

"Then you will be the money-lender for my money!" said the woodsman with delight. "When will you want the cash?"

"This very night."

"Done!" said the devil.

"Done!" said Tom Walker. So they shook hands and struck a bargain.

In a few days' time, Tom Walker was seated behind a desk in Boston. He soon became known as a man with ready money.

Times were hard when Tom Walker first set up his money-lending business. His door was crowded with customers. In came the needy, the dreamers, and shopkeepers who were afraid of losing their shops. In short—everyone who was desperate for money hurried to Tom Walker.

Tom called himself the "friend of the needy." But the more a person needed money, the harder were Tom's terms. He piled up mortgages and squeezed out of his customers everything that they owned. At length, he would send them— dry as a sponge—away from his door.

7 In this way, Tom Walker made money hand over hand. He became a rich and mighty man. As is usual, he built himself a huge house. But it was mostly for show.

He was too cheap to furnish the greater part of it. He rode in a costly carriage— but he nearly starved the horses that pulled it. In truth, he enjoyed nothing and he took care of nothing. The ungreased wheels of his carriage groaned and screeched as he drove to his office every morning. That awful sound might have been the crying souls of the poor people he was squeezing.

As Tom got older, however, he began to think. Having gathered up all the good things of this world, he began to worry about those of the next. He was sorry he had made the bargain with his cloaked friend. Now he began to think about ways to get out of the deal.

It was then that Tom Walker became a churchgoer. He prayed loudly, as if heaven were to be won by the force of his lungs. Indeed, the one who had sinned the most during the week said his Sunday prayers in the loudest voice.

Tom kept his eye on his neighbors, too. He seemed to think that *their* sins would help him through the gates of heaven.

But in spite of all his praying and church-going, Tom had a terrible feeling. He feared that the devil, after all, would have his due. It is said that he always carried a small Bible in his coat pocket. He did this so that he might not be caught off guard. He also had a big Bible on his desk. When people called on business, he would often be found reading it. At such times he would carefully lay his glasses in the book to mark his place. Then he would turn around to make some greedy bargain.

Some say that Tom grew a little hare-brained in his old days. They say that, when his horse died, he had the animal saddled and buried with its feet pointed up. He supposed that at the last day the world would be turned upside-down. In that case, his horse would be all set for riding.

Tom was getting ready to give his old friend the devil a run for it. The story about the horse may not have been true. If Tom really did such a thing, it didn't

work. At least, so says the real story—
which ended in the following way:

It was a hot afternoon in late summer.
A big thunder storm was coming up. Tom
sat at his desk, wearing his white night
cap and silk morning-gown. He was on
the point of laying claim to someone's
home. This would complete the ruin of a
fellow whom he had always called his
friend. The poor man begged Tom for a
few more months to pay. But Tom refused
him even one more day.

"My family will be ruined!" cried the
fellow.

"I must take care of myself in these
hard times," answered Tom.

"But you have already taken all my
money from me," the man cried.

Tom grew angry. "The devil take me,"
said he, "if I have made a cent!"

Just then there were three loud knocks
at the street door. Tom stepped out to see
who was there. He saw the big cloaked
man, holding a black horse. It stamped
its hooves as if ready to go.

"Tom, you're come for," said the cloaked fellow. Tom stepped back—but too late. He had left his little Bible in the bottom of his coat pocket. The big Bible on the desk was buried under his papers. Never was a sinner so poorly prepared!

The cloaked man hurried Tom into the saddle. He lashed the whip, and away the horse ran—with Tom on his back in the middle of a thunder storm. People stared at him from their windows. Away went Tom Walker, racing down the streets! His white cap bobbed up and down. His morning gown waved in the wind. At every step, the horse struck fire out of the ground. When people behind their windows turned to look for the cloaked man, he had disappeared.

Tom Walker never returned. A fellow who lived on the edge of the swamp said that he had seen him. At the height of the storm, he said he had heard the pounding of hooves and a howling sound from the road. The man hurried to the window.

There he saw a dark figure on a horse that ran like mad across the fields. Over the hills it went, and down into the black swamp toward the old Indian fort. Shortly after, lightning flashed in that direction, the fellow said. It seemed to set the whole forest on fire.

The good people of Boston shook their heads and shrugged their shoulders. They were used to stories about witches and ghosts. Tricks of the devil had been common since the first settlement of the colony. They were not so much horror-struck as might have been expected.

Someone was chosen to take charge of Tom's business. But there was nothing, it turned out, to take charge of. When his office was searched, all of his papers were found to have turned to ashes. In place of gold and silver, his iron chest was filled with wood chips and shavings. Two piles of bones lay in his stable in the place of his hungry horses. The very next day, his great house caught fire and burned to the ground.

Such was the end of Tom Walker and his ill-gotten riches.

Let all greedy money-lenders take this story to heart—for it is true. To this day you can see the very hole under the oak trees where Tom dug up Kidd's money. Some people say that the swamp and the old Indian fort are even now haunted on stormy nights. They say that a figure on horseback, wearing morning-gown and white cap, can still be seen there. Surely it is the troubled spirit of the money-lender.

Over time, this story became quite well known. It led to the popular saying that is so often heard in New England. There, just the words, "The Devil and Tom Walker," are a frightening reminder of the dangers of greed.

The Specter Bridegroom

What if the wrong groom turns up at a wedding? Would the bride be willing to marry him anyway? But why would anyone want to marry a ghost?

UNDER HER AUNTS' TEACHINGS SHE HAD LEARNED
EVERYTHING THAT A FINE LADY NEEDS TO KNOW.

The Specter Bridegroom

A castle once stood high on a hill in a wild part of upper Germany. It had belonged to the Baron Von Landshort. Now the ruin of the old castle was almost buried among the trees. Only its old watch tower could still be seen.

The baron was a part of the great family of Katzenellenbogen. Most of the German nobles had left their castles. They had built new homes in the valleys, closer to the rest of the world. Still, the baron stayed proudly in his castle on the hill. And he made sure to continue some of the old family feuds. He got along poorly with many of his neighbors because of fights between their great-great-grandfathers.

The baron had but one child, a daughter. All her nurses and cousins adored her. They told her father that she was the most beautiful girl in all of Germany. And who should know better than they? She had been brought up by two aunts. Under their teachings she had learned everything that a fine lady needs to know. By the time she was 18, she could sew beautifully and read very well. She could spell and she could write. Why, she could even sign her own name without missing a single letter.

The aunts watched over their niece very closely. She never went beyond the castle alone. And, as to men... pah! Without her family's nod, she would not give a look to even the handsomest man in the world. No, not even if he were dying right at her feet.

The girl was blooming into a lovely woman. She was like a perfect rose blushing forth among guardian thorns. Bad luck might bring other girls to no good. But nothing of the kind, thank heaven, could happen to the daughter of Katzenellenbogen.

The baron was a small man with a large soul. He loved to tell stories. Happily, he found no better listeners than those who ate at his table. His favorite tales were about ghosts.

At the time of this story, there was a great gathering at the castle. It was held to welcome the bridegroom of the baron's daughter. The marriage agreement had been made between the baron and an old nobleman of Bavaria. The young people were promised to one another without ever having met.

The future bridegroom was a young man named Count Von Altenburg. He had been called away from the army just for this event. A message from him had arrived at the castle. His letter told the exact day and hour he would arrive.

The castle was busy preparing his welcome. The baron buzzed about. He was as restless as a fly on a warm summer's day. The kitchen was crowded with good cheer. Everything was ready for the honored guest—but the guest did not arrive.

Hour after hour rolled by. The baron climbed to the high tower. He wanted to be the first to catch sight of the count. The sun set. The bats began to fly by. The road grew darker.

The old castle of Landshort was in a state of worry. But, meanwhile, some interesting things were happening not far away.

The young Count Von Altenburg was peacefully making his way along the road. At Wurzburg, he had met a friend named Herman Von Starkenfaust. The young count had served with him in the army and knew him well. His father's castle was not far from the castle of Landshort. In fact, an old-time feud had kept those families quarreling through the years.

In the happy moment of meeting, the young friends remembered all their past adventures. The count told his friend about his coming marriage. He said that he had never seen the young lady, but that he'd heard of her beauty and charms.

Because the friends were going the same direction, they decided to ride along together. Soon they happily set off from Wurzburg.

Together they entered the mountains. Before long they crossed a very lonely and thickly wooded mountain pass. Now everybody knows about the forests of Germany. They have always been as filled with robbers as Germany's castles are by ghosts! Alas, the travelers were attacked.

The two noblemen fought bravely indeed. But they were overpowered. By the time the robbers ran off, the count had been badly hurt. His friend carefully carried him back to the city of Wurzburg. But it was clear that the days of the poor count were numbered.

With his dying breath, the count asked his friend to go quickly to the castle of Landshort. Please explain, he begged, the reason why he had not kept his date with his bride. "Unless this is done," he said, "I shall not sleep quietly in my grave!" The faithful Starkenfaust promised to do as he was asked.

Starkenfaust shed a tear over the death of his friend. His head spun as he thought about the job that lay ahead. He had to present himself at Landshort— an uninvited guest and the son of an enemy family! And even worse, he had to bring terrible news.

Still, there were certain whisperings in the back of his mind. He *did* want to see this girl for himself. Who would *not* want to see this rare beauty of Katzenellenbogen who had been shut away from the rest of the world? Starkenfaust liked the ladies almost as much as he liked a good adventure.

Before he left, he helped plan the funeral of his friend. The count was to be buried in the church of Wurzburg.

The family of Katzenellenbogen knew nothing of this, of course. The guests at the castle were still waiting for their guest and for their dinner. The baron was still airing himself on the watch tower.

When night closed in, the honored guest still had not arrived. The baron came down from the tower. The dinner could no longer be put off. The meats were already overcooked. So the baron gave orders to start dinner without the guest. They were just about to begin eating when a horn sounded from the gate. The baron hurried out to meet his future son-in-law.

A tall soldier on a black horse stood before the gate. His face was pale.

"I am sorry," said the stranger, "to break in upon you this way...."

But the baron stopped him with many words of welcome. The stranger could not get another word in. So he bowed his head and listened in silence. By the time the baron took a breath, they were inside the castle. The stranger was about to speak again when the two aunts led forth the bride. He looked at her for only a moment, and he was charmed. He could not turn away from her lovely form. As for the lady herself, a sweet smile played about her lips. After all, she was a girl of 18, ready for love. It was impossible for her not to be pleased with so fine-looking a young man.

The hour was late. The baron hurried everyone into dinner. The feast was served up in the great hall of the castle. But the young man had eyes only for the bride. He whispered into her ear. His face looked very serious. The lady's color came and went as she listened with deep attention. It was clear that the young couple had fallen deeply in love.

The dinner went on merrily. The baron told his best stories. But among all the merry-making, the honored guest was strangely grim. His face looked even sadder as the evening passed. At times he was lost in thought. His talk with the bride became more and more serious and mysterious. His face clouded. Her body trembled.

All this could not escape the notice of the company. Their laughter died down. The stories became gloomier. One fair lady almost fainted from fright at the tale of a goblin horseman.

But the bridegroom listened to this tale with interest. The moment the story was finished, he sighed and said good-bye to the company.

"What?" cried the baron. "You are going to leave the castle at midnight? Why, a bed is all ready for you."

The stranger answered sadly, "I must lay my head upon a different bed tonight." Then he walked slowly out of the hall. The maiden aunts were both confused and frightened. The bride hung her head. A tear came into her eye.

The baron followed Starkenfaust to the court of the castle. There his black horse stood pawing the earth. The young man addressed the baron in a hollow tone.

"Now that we are alone," he said, "I will tell you the reason for my going. There is a place that I must be—a date I cannot break."

"Can't you send someone in your place?" asked the baron.

"No. I must be there in person. My presence is required at the Wurzburg church."

"Yes," said the baron. "But not until tomorrow. Tomorrow you shall take your bride there."

"No! No!" replied the stranger. "My date is not with a bride. It is with the worms! I am a dead man. I have been killed by robbers. My body lies at Wurzburg. At midnight I am to be buried. The grave is waiting for me!"

With that he jumped on his horse. The sound of hooves was soon lost in the whistling of the night wind.

The baron returned to the hall. He told his guests what had been said. Two ladies fainted. Others fell sick at the thought of having dined with a ghost—a specter. And anyone who might have doubted the story had no doubts at all the next day. At dawn, word arrived of the young count's murder and his burial at Wurzburg church.

The poor bride-to-be! She filled the house with her sobs.

Two days passed. The sad young lady had gone to her bedroom for the night. As always, her aunts stayed with her. But that night the niece could not sleep. The clock had just chimed midnight when soft music came from the garden. The young lady left her bed and stepped to the window.

There she saw a tall figure standing among the shadows of the trees. As the figure raised its head, moonlight fell upon its face. Heaven and earth! She beheld the Specter Bridegroom! A loud scream cut the air. Her aunt, awakened by the music, had followed her to the window. When the young lady looked again, the specter had disappeared.

The aunt was beside herself in terror. But the young lady found something sweet even in the specter of her lover. The aunt declared that she would never sleep in that room again. The niece declared as strongly that she would sleep in no other room in the castle. So it was that the young woman had to sleep alone. She begged her aunt to keep the specter's visit a secret.

For a whole week, the good lady kept her promise. That was not easy for the old woman. Indeed, she dearly loved to talk and had *such* a story to tell! But then one morning, alarming news was brought to the breakfast table. The daughter was not to be found. Her bed had not been slept in. The window was open.

The poor aunt wrung her hands and wept. "The goblin!" she cried. "She's been carried away by the goblin!"

Then she broke her promise to the young lady. In a few words she told of the fearful scene in the garden. The Specter Bridegroom must have carried away his bride!

The poor baron! What a heart-breaking day for a fond father! He called for his horse. He would go out himself to find his poor girl.

But just then a lady was seen riding toward the castle. She galloped up to the gate, sprang from her horse, and fell at the baron's feet. It was his lost daughter! And who was at her side but the Specter Bridegroom! The baron looked at his daughter and then at the specter. The young man no longer looked so pale and serious. His face, in fact, was bright with joy.

The mystery was soon cleared up. The young man announced himself as Sir Herman Von Starkenfaust. (As you must have known all the while, he was no goblin at all.) Now he told about his adventures with the young count. He explained that he had hurried to the castle to deliver the sad news. He reminded the baron that he could not get a word in through the old man's greetings.

Starkenfaust said that the sight of the bride had left him unable to think of anything but her. He confessed that the baron's goblin stories had given him an idea. Fearing the baron's dislike for his family, he had secretly visited the young lady's garden. After "haunting" her window, he had wooed her, won her, and carried her away. And, last night, he had wed her!

The baron might have been angry. But he loved his daughter and felt only joy at her return. It was true, of course, that her husband was of an unfriendly house. But at least, thank Heaven, he was not a goblin. That was something!

On the spot, the baron forgave the young couple. Then the celebrations began again. It is true that the aunts felt that they had failed in guarding the daughter. And one of them was quite upset because her wonderful story was ruined. The only specter she ever saw had turned out to be a fake! But the niece seemed perfectly happy that he was real flesh and blood. And so the story ends.

Thinking About
the Stories

Rip Van Winkle

1. Who is the main character in this story? Who are one or two of the minor characters? Describe each of these characters in one or two sentences.

2. What period of time is covered in this story—an hour, a week, several years? What role, if any, does time play in the story?

3. The plot is the series of events that takes place in a story. Usually, story events are linked in some way. Can you name an event in this story that was the cause of a later event?

The Devil and Tom Walker

1. Is there a hero in this story? A villain? Who are they? What did these characters do or say to form your opinion?

2. Many stories are meant to teach a lesson of some kind. Is the author trying to make a point in this story? What is it?

3. Suppose this story had a completely different outcome. Can you think of another effective ending for this story?

The Specter Bridegroom

1. An author builds the plot around the conflict in a story. In this story, what forces or characters are struggling against each other? How is the conflict finally resolved?

2. Look back at the illustration that introduces this story. What character or characters are pictured? What is happening in the scene? What clues does the picture give you about the time and place of the story?

3. Interesting story plots often have unexpected twists and turns. What surprises did you find in this story?